AFRICAN AMERICANS in Politics
A BOOK OF POSTCARDS

THE SCHOMBURG CENTER FOR RESEARCH IN BLACK CULTURE

THE NEW YORK PUBLIC LIBRARY

Pomegranate

SAN FRANCISCO

Pomegranate Communications, Inc.
Box 808022, Petaluma CA 94975
800 227 1428; www.pomegranate.com

Pomegranate Europe Ltd.
Unit 1, Heathcote Business Centre, Hurlbutt Road
Warwick, Warwickshire CV34 6TD, UK
[+44] 0 1926 430111; sales@pomeurope.co.uk

ISBN 978-0-7649-4872-5
Pomegranate Catalog No. AA586

Pomegranate publishes books of postcards on a wide range of subjects.
Please contact the publisher for more information.

Cover designed by Gina Bostian
Printed in Korea
18 17 16 15 14 13 12 11 10 09   10 9 8 7 6 5 4 3 2 1

To facilitate detachment of the postcards from this book, fold each card along its perforation line before tearing.

Before

Before Barack Obama, there were many heroes in the African American struggle to gain a voice in the nation's political process. Crispus Attucks, Frederick Douglass, the 54th Massachusetts Infantry Regiment, Mary McLeod Bethune, Adam Clayton Powell Jr., and a host of others fought to make America and American democracy real for all of the country's citizens. Like Attucks, people of African descent were there at the founding of the nation. And since then, millions have fought, bled, and died to help define, defend, and protect the lofty ideals embodied in the Declaration of Independence, the U.S. Constitution, and the Bill of Rights. Spanning more than 200 years, *African Americans in Politics* is a brief survey of that quest.

Prior to 1866, most African Americans were not permitted to participate in the American democratic process. They could neither vote nor hold office nor serve on juries. But their presence helped define the nation and determine its development. For a brief period following the Civil War, constitutional amendments granted blacks citizenship and the right to vote, providing them their first significant opportunity to participate in the governance of this country. Thousands voted and hundreds were elected to local, state, and national office. By the 1880s the gains of the preceding two decades were largely lost. Not until the 1970s would significant numbers of blacks be elected to public office.

Since the 1960s several people of African descent—women as well as men—have set their sights on the presidency of the United States. Dick Gregory, Shirley Chisholm, Jesse Jackson, Carol Moseley Braun, Al Sharpton, Alan Keyes, and Barack Obama campaigned for the nomination of their respective parties. With his historic victory in the 2008 election, President Obama stands on the shoulders of all of those who struggled within and outside of the political establishment to advance the causes of freedom, justice, equality, and human dignity for African Americans and all of humankind.

AFRICAN AMERICANS IN POLITICS

Democratic presidential hopeful Carol Moseley Braun speaking
at the Brown and Black Presidential Forum, Des Moines, IA,
January 11, 2004
Photographer: Charlie Neibergall
AP/Wide World Photos, as seen in the Schomburg Center for
Research in Black Culture exhibition, "African Americans and
American Politics." All rights reserved.

AFRICAN AMERICANS IN POLITICS

Democratic presidential candidate Senator Barack Obama (D-IL)
waves to supporters before speaking at a primary night rally,
St. Paul, MN, June 3, 2008.
Photographer: Morry Gash
AP/Wide World Photos, as seen in the Schomburg Center for
Research in Black Culture exhibition, "African Americans and
American Politics." All rights reserved.

707 782 9000   WWW.POMEGRANATE.COM

Pomegranate

AFRICAN AMERICANS IN POLITICS

The Fifteenth Amendment
Artist: James C. Beard, 1870
Photographs and Prints

WWW.POMEGRANATE.COM

707 782 9000

Pomegranate

Engraved by J.C. Buttre

Frederick Douglass.

African Americans in Politics

Portrait of Frederick Douglass
Engraving by J. C. Buttre, c. 1850
Photographs and Prints

707 782 9000   WWW.POMEGRANATE.COM

Pomegranate

AFRICAN AMERICANS IN POLITICS

Dr. Martin Luther King Jr. speaking at the National Conference for
a New Politics (NCNP) Convention, Chicago, IL, August 31, 1967
Photograph © Benedict J. Fernandez
© The Estate of Martin Luther King Jr. Collection of the Schomburg
Center for Research in Black Culture. All rights reserved.

707 782 9000   WWW.POMEGRANATE.COM

Pomegranate

HARPER'S WEEKLY.

A JOURNAL OF CIVILIZATION

Vol. XI.—No. 568.]

NEW YORK, SATURDAY, NOVEMBER 16, 1867.

Entered according to Act of Congress, in the Year 1867, by Harper & Brothers, in the Clerk's Office of the District Court for the Southern District of New York.

[SINGLE COPIES TEN CENTS.
[$4.00 PER YEAR IN ADVANCE.

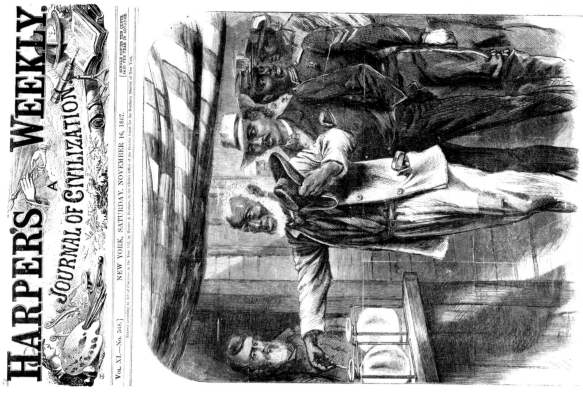

THE FIRST VOTE.—DRAWN BY A. R. WAUD.—[SEE NEXT PAGE.]

AFRICAN AMERICANS IN POLITICS

The First Vote
Artist: A. R. Waud
Published in *Harper's Weekly,* November 16, 1867
Photographs and Prints

AFRICAN AMERICANS IN POLITICS

Colored Women Voters Organization, Georgia, c. 1925
Photographer unknown
Photographs and Prints

WWW.POMEGRANATE.COM

707 782 9000

Pomegranate

AFRICAN AMERICANS IN POLITICS

Democratic presidential hopeful Rev. Jesse Jackson speaking at
the White House, January 4, 1984. Behind Jackson is President
Ronald Reagan.
Photographer: Barry Thurma
AP/Wide World Photos, as seen in the Schomburg Center for
Research in Black Culture exhibition, "African Americans and
American Politics."

WWW.POMEGRANATE.COM

707 782 9000

Pomegranate

AFRICAN AMERICANS IN POLITICS

Commerce Secretary Ron Brown, chairman of the Democratic
Party, gavels the opening of the Democratic National
Convention in New York City, July 14, 1992.
Photographer: Ron Edmonds
AP/Wide World Photos, as seen in the Schomburg Center for
Research in Black Culture exhibition, "African Americans and
American Politics."

707 782 9000   WWW.POMEGRANATE.COM

Pomegranate

AFRICAN AMERICANS IN POLITICS

Democratic presidential hopeful Senator Barack Obama (D-IL) and his wife, Michelle, arrive at an election night rally, St. Paul, MN, June 3, 2008.
Photographer: Chris Carlson
AP/Wide World Photos, as seen in the Schomburg Center for Research in Black Culture exhibition, "African Americans and American Politics." All rights reserved.

707 782 9000   WWW.POMEGRANATE.COM

Pomegranate

African Americans in Politics

Congresswoman Barbara Jordan
Photographer: Dev O'Neill
Photographs and Prints

WWW.POMEGRANATE.COM

707 782 9000

Pomegranate

AFRICAN AMERICANS IN POLITICS

The "Black Cabinet" during President Franklin Delano
Roosevelt's administration, 1938
Photographer: Scurlock Studio
Scurlock Studio Collection, National Museum of American
History, Smithsonian Institution Archives Center
Photographs and Prints

707 782 9000   WWW.POMEGRANATE.COM

Pomegranate

African Americans in Politics

The Boston Massacre, March 5th 1770
Lithograph by J. H. Bufford, c. 1856,
after W. Champney
Photographs and Prints

WWW.POMEGRANATE.COM

707 782 9000

Pomegranate

COME AND JOIN US BROTHERS.

PUBLISHED BY THE SUPERVISORY COMMITTEE FOR RECRUITING COLORED REGIMENTS

1210 CHESTNUT ST. PHILADELPHIA.

African Americans in Politics

Come and Join Us Brothers
Union recruitment poster, 1863
Photographs and Prints

WWW.POMEGRANATE.COM

707 782 9000

Pomegranate

AFRICAN AMERICANS IN POLITICS

General Colin Powell, former U.S. Secretary of State
Photographer unknown
Photographs and Prints

WWW.POMEGRANATE.COM

707 782 9000

Pomegranate

African Americans in Politics

The forty-three-member Congressional Black Caucus, 2008 CBC Photo, as seen in the Schomburg Center for Research in Black Culture exhibition, "African Americans and American Politics."

707 782 9000   WWW.POMEGRANATE.COM

Pomegranate

AFRICAN AMERICANS IN POLITICS

Senator Edward Brooke
Photographer unknown
Photographs and Prints

707 782 9000   WWW.POMEGRANATE.COM

Pomegranate

African Americans in Politics

Reading the Emancipation Proclamation
Illustrator: H. W. Herrick
Photographs and Prints

707 782 9000   WWW.POMEGRANATE.COM

Pomegranate

Entered according to act of Congress in the year 1872 by Currier & Ives in the Office of the Librarian of Congress at Washington

ROBERT C. DE LARGE, M.C. of S. Carolina.　　　JEFFERSON H. LONG, M.C. of Georgia.

U.S. Senator H.R. REVELS, of Mississippi　　BENJ. S. TURNER, M.C. of Alabama.　　JOSIAH T. WALLS, M.C. of Florida.　　JOSEPH H. RAINY, M.C. of S. Carolina.　　R. BROWN ELLIOT, M.C. of S. Carolina.

THE FIRST COLORED SENATOR AND REPRESENTATIVES.

In the 41st and 42nd Congress of the United States.

NEW YORK. PUBLISHED BY CURRIER & IVES, 125 NASSAU STREET.

AFRICAN AMERICANS IN POLITICS

The First Colored Senator and Representatives in the 41st and 42nd Congress of the United States
Artists: Currier & Ives, New York
Published in *Harper's Weekly*, c. 1872
Photographs and Prints

WWW.POMEGRANATE.COM

707 782 9000

Pomegranate

AFRICAN AMERICANS IN POLITICS

Mississippi delegation, National Black Political Convention,
Gary, IN, March 10–12, 1972
Photographer: Robert A. Sengstacke
Image © 1972 Robert Abbott Sengstacke. Collection of the
Schomburg Center for Research in Black Culture. All rights
reserved.

707 782 9000   WWW.POMEGRANATE.COM

Pomegranate

African Americans in Politics

They marched together for equality and the dream.
Organizers of the March on Washington pose before the Lincoln
Memorial, 1963. Back row (left to right): Mathew Ahmann,
Rabbi Joachim Prinz, John Lewis, Dr. Eugene P. Donnaly, Floyd
McKissick, Walter Reuther. Front row (left to right): Whitney
Young, Cleveland Robinson, A. Philip Randolph, Dr. Martin
Luther King Jr., Roy Wilkins
Photograph by Bertrand H. Miles, courtesy of Susann and
Jennifer L. Miles
Photographs and Prints

WWW.POMEGRANATE.COM

707 782 9000

Pomegranate

EX-SENATOR BRUCE   HON. FREDERICK DOUGLASS   EX-SENATOR REVELS

HEROES OF THE COLORED RACE.

AFRICAN AMERICANS IN POLITICS

Heroes of the Colored Race
Lithograph, 1881
Artist: J. Hoover
Most prominently featured are Blanche K. Bruce, Frederick
Douglass, and Hiram Revels.
Arts and Artifacts

707 782 9000   WWW.POMEGRANATE.COM

Pomegranate

AFRICAN AMERICANS IN POLITICS

Members of the National Negro Congress picket against
discriminatory hiring practices by defense contractors, c. 1943.
Photographer: Scurlock Studio
Scurlock Studio Collection, National Museum of American
History, Smithsonian Institution Archives Center
Photographs and Prints

707 782 9000   WWW.POMEGRANATE.COM

Pomegranate

P. B. S. PINCHBACK

Lieutenant Governor and Acting Governor of Louisiana
and United States Senator Elect

AFRICAN AMERICANS IN POLITICS

Portrait of P. B. S. Pinchback
Photographer unknown
Photographs and Prints

707 782 9000   WWW.POMEGRANATE.COM

Pomegranate

CONSTITUTION

AND

PROCEEDINGS

OF THE

FIRST ANNUAL CONVENTION

OF THE

PEOPLE OF COLOUR,

HELD BY ADJOURNMENTS IN THE

CITY OF PHILADELPHIA,

FROM THE

Sixth to the Eleventh of June,

INCLUSIVE,

1831.

———

PHILADELPHIA:

PUBLISHED BY ORDER OF THE COMMITTEE
OF ARRANGEMENTS.

———

AFRICAN AMERICANS IN POLITICS

Minutes and Proceedings of the First Annual Convention of the People of Color

Published in the *Salem Gazette*, 1831
Manuscripts, Archives and Rare Books

WWW.POMEGRANATE.COM

707 782 9000

Pomegranate

African Americans in Politics

Adam Clayton Powell Jr. campaigns for Congress in Harlem, c. 1945.
Photograph by Austin Hansen, used with permission of Joyce
Hansen and the Schomburg Center
Image © Austin Hansen Photographic Collection. Collection of
the Schomburg Center for Research in Black Culture. All rights
reserved.

WWW.POMEGRANATE.COM

707 782 9000

Pomegranate

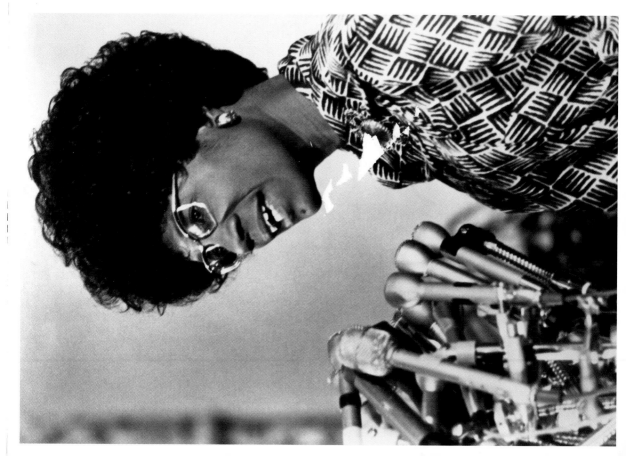

AFRICAN AMERICANS IN POLITICS

Shirley Chisholm announces her candidacy for
the U.S. House of Representatives, 1968.
Photograph: U.S. House of Representatives
Photographs and Prints

WWW.POMEGRANATE.COM

707 782 9000

Pomegranate

STORMING FORT WAGNER.

AFRICAN AMERICANS IN POLITICS

Storming Fort Wagner; Charge of the 54th Massachusetts Colored Regiment, July 18, 1863
Lithograph, 1890
Artist unknown
Arts and Artifacts

WWW.POMEGRANATE.COM

707 782 9000

Pomegranate

AFRICAN AMERICANS IN POLITICS

The Thirteenth Amendment, December 18, 1865
Manuscripts, Archives and Rare Books

WWW.POMEGRANATE.COM

707 782 9000

Pomegranate